Ralph Broome

An Examination of the Expediency of Continuing the Present Impeachment

Ralph Broome

An Examination of the Expediency of Continuing the Present Impeachment

ISBN/EAN: 9783337337896

Printed in Europe, USA, Canada, Australia, Japan

Cover: Foto ©Suzi / pixelio.de

More available books at **www.hansebooks.com**

EXAMINATION

OF THE

EXPEDIENCY

OF CONTINUING THE PRESENT

IMPEACHMENT;

BY

RALPH BROOME, Esq.

AUTHOR OF THE ELUCIDATION OF THE
ARTICLES OF IMPEACHMENT

AGAINST

WARREN HASTINGS, Esq.

―――――――――――

LONDON:

Printed for JOHN STOCKDALE, oppofite Burlington
Houfe, Piccadilly.

M.DCC.XCI.

[Price Two Shillings and Six-pence.]

PRECEDENTS

ON

IMPEACHMENTS.

This Day is Publifhed.

IN ONE VOLUME OCTAVO,

Price Five Shillings in Boards,

A N

ELUCIDATION

OF THE ARTICLES OF

IMPEACHMENT,

Preferred by the laft PARLIAMENT againft

WARREN HASTINGS, Esq.

B Y

RALP.H BROOME, Esq.

Captain in the Service of the EAST INDIA COMPANY
on the Bengal Eftablifhment, and Perfian Tranflator
to the Army on the Frontier ftation, during Part of
the late War in India.

N. B. At the latter End of this WORK is Con-
tained a View of all the Precedents relative to the Continuance and Abatement of Impeachments on the Diffolution of Parliament, with an Examination of the Arguments pro and con.

LONDON

Printed for JOHN STOCKDALE, Piccadilly.

COMPLETE EDITION

OF

SIMKIN's LETTERS,

CONTAINING A PARTICULAR ACCOUNT OF

Mr. HASTINGS's TRIAL

From its commencement in 1778, to the prefent Time.

This Day is Publifhed,

Beautifully printed on a Superfine Wire wove PAPER, in One
Volume Octavo, Price 7s. in Boards,

THE

LETTERS

OF

SIMKIN THE SECOND,

POETIC RECORDER OF ALL THE

PROCEEDINGS

UPON THE TRIAL OF

WARREN HASTINGS, Esq.

IN WESTMINSTER HALL.

I—— curre per Alpes,
Ut PUERIS *placeas et* DECLAMATIO *fias!*
 JUVENAL.

Enligbæn'd Statefman! go through Toil and Strife,
And for thy Country's Good, embroil thy Life.
Go—*migbty Warrior!*—wide and wider roam,
To come at length, and be abus'd at home. ANON.

London: Printed for JOHN STOCKDALE.

January 8th, 1791.

N. B. The Second Part of the above Work may be had feparate to
complete the firft Edition in One fmall Volume 8vo. Price 3s. in
Boards.

AN

EXAMINATION,

&c.

I HAVE upon former occasions addressed the public upon the subject of the present Impeachment. What I have written has been collected by Mr. Stockdale, and sold in the shape of a pamphlet. The collection has been reviewed by the monthly and literary reviewers; the former paid me the compliment of saying, that I had rendered that intelligible, which had, till then, baffled the powers of comprehension; and the latter said, that the arguments I had made use

B of

of were weighty, and deferving of confideration.

Thus encouraged, I venture to lay before the public fome reflections upon the
prefent ftate of the impeachment above mentioned. It was, till very lately, my decided
opinion founded upon fearch of precedents,
that the proceedings would abate or be an-
nihilated by the diffolution of the laft Parliament. In that opinion I find myfelf, as far
as refpects the Houfe of Commons, totally
miftaken; but I have this confolation, that
I have erred in company with the moft refpectable law authorities in this kingdom.
Much ingenuity has been made ufe of to
eftablifh the validity of the precedent in
1678, and to deftroy the effect of all thofe
that followed. This much, however, ftands
uncontradicted and uncontroverted by any
one. Except the inftances that occurred
between the years 1678 and 1685, the
whole Hiftory of England cannot furnifh a

pre-

precedent of an impeachment begun by one
Parliament and purfued by another. The
cafes of Lords Peterborough and Salifbury
and the Duke of Leeds, are reprefented as
particular cafes, and having no analogy to
the prefent ; but for my own part I cannot
difcover any other diffimilarity than that of
rank. The cafes above mentioned have
nobility, members of the upper Houfe, for
the accufed, and the prefent cafe has a lefs
dignified fubject, a Commoner only. Whether it be among the privileges of the Peer-
age that the diffolution of Parliament fhall
extinguifh the impeachment of a Peer, I
know not, but it certainly was not put upon
that footing. The judgement of the Lords
in the cafes of Lord Danby, Peterborough,
and 'Salifbury, in the years 1685 and
in 1690, was declared to have for its foundation, the laws of the land and the ufage
of Parliament, without even an infinuation
of exclufive peculiarity in favour of their
own body. There are, I admit, many pe-

B 2　　　　　　　culiarities

culiarities in the cafe of Mr. Haftings, which diftinguifh it from all ftate trials in this country, or in any other. Among thefe peculiarities may be reckoned the length of time fince the facts happened, the duration of the trial, and the feverity with which it has been conducted. Were we to eftimate the degrees of guilt by the length of the fpeeches made againft him, by the harfhnefs of the epithets with which they are loaded, by the number of days employed totally in the arts of aggravation, and by the duration of the impeachment, we could not fail to confider him as the worft of mankind; as one who had ruined his country, nay, as the common enemy of human nature. If any man writes or fpeaks in his favour, he is called an hireling or a partaker of the plunder, or he is ftigmatized with fome other appellation equally opprobrious. Some of thofe who, being called by the Managers, gave teftimony in Mr. Haftings's favour, were either directly or indirectly accufed of

per-

perjury, and I believe every witnefs without exception, who happened to fpeak in his
favour, was reprefented to the world as a
very fufpicious character. On the contrary, thofe witneffes whofe teftimony tended
to criminate, were extolled as men of un-
queftionable veracity, of the pureft honour,
and moft inflexible morality.

When Mr. Paterfon's report concerning the
infurrection at Rungpore, and the crueltie
committed by Deby Sing, was dilated on
in Weftminfter Hall, he was reprefented
as a young gentleman of more than apofto-
lic credit and veracity. But fince the fame
young gentleman, hearing of the unfair ufe
which had been made of that report, and of
its being perverted to the purpofes of calumny, has written home declaring his abhorrence thereof, and that Mr. Haftings, fo
far from promoting or protecting guilt, was
the moft forward for detecting and avenging
it, we hear nothing more of his extraordinary

nary qualities and uncommon attachment to the caufe of truth and juftice.

I have looked into the hiftory of our own country, where I found many examples of violent and eager profecutions for ftate crimes ; fome of them have been fpeedily brought to an iffue, fatal to the objects of accufation ; but there is not one inftance to be found, wherein time has not operated to the abatement of public anger and profecution. Lord Bolingbroke was attainted for high treafon, and afterwards pardoned. Lord Oxford was put upon his trial for a fimilar offence ; he was accufed of having bafely betrayed the intereft of his country, and having affifted her enemies. Crimes, greater than thefe, if true, could not be committed by a minifter or ftatefman, yet we find that the profecution and punifhment of this offender was not thought of confequence equal to the prefervation of formal etiquette. The Commons of that day, foon-

er

er than fuffer the judges of the higheft court
of judicature in this kingdom, to exercife
that right and privilege which muft neceffarily belong to every court of juftice, viz.
that of fettling the form of proceeding,
abandoned the profecution altogether. Many
other inftances may be adduced of thofe
who have done the moft effectual and moft
permanent injuries to their country, and yet
have owed their fafety to the diffolution of
Parliament, or to the lapfe of time. But
none of thofe things which operated to the
prefervation of thofe who injured their
country, are permitted to operate in the favour of him who has moft effectually ferved
her. Time, inftead of cooling, inflames
refentment, and the ghoft of the Parliament
that is dead, rifes up to re-kindle and ani-
mate the vengeance of that which is living.
Precedents are laid afide, analogy is difre-
garded, and eftablifhed legal opinions are
contradicted. One day we are told, that
the profecution of the Houfe of Commons

is

is the profecution of the people of England,, and the next day we hear that every repre- fentative is totally independent of his confti- tuents. If the people petition to the rulers of their own creation, their petitions are rejected; but if the name of the people is, made ufe of for form's fake only, they are indiffolubly bound and inextricably impli- cated in the acts of their uncontrolable re- prefentatives. According to the doctrine of this day, the refolutions of a paft Houfe of Commons are binding upon the prefent, and the dying requeft of a diffolved body ought to be regarded by their fucceffors with all the reverence and veneration of a pious fon, to the admonitions of a departed father. Pofterity in reading the hiftory of the pre- fent times will naturally inquire into the caufe of thefe extraordinary doctrines and events. They will fay, what crime had the man committed, or what acts of uncom- mon atrocity had he been guilty of, that the old cuftoms and ufage of Parliament

I were

were to be set aside for the special purpose
of punishing his offences? And all this in
a country where such strict regard is paid
to form and ceremony, that many of the
most guilty wretches are suffered to avail
themselves of some trifling technical error,
and thereby escape with their lives and for-
tunes from the hands of justice. Upon inquiry, they will find nothing but what unavoidably arose from circumstances and situ-
ation; that supposing the acts were intrin-
sically wrong, they were done, not with a
view to serve himself or his dependents, but
for the indispensably necessary service of
that very nation which now prosecutes him;
a nation, that, if there were any thing
wrong in the conduct of Mr. Hastings,
participate, nay, appropriate the guilt to
themselves, by keeping possession of what
he is said to have taken unjustly from the
natives of India. But I think I have demonstrated in the work which I alluded
to, in the first page, to the satisfaction of

C   every

every candid reader, that the taxing of Cheyt
Sing in the time of war, and the advising of
the Nabob to confiscate the treasure of which
his mother unjustly and unnaturally deprived
him, and afterwards turned against him, were
perfectly agreeable to the laws and customs
of Indostan, and as reconcilable to the principles of sound policy and strict justice, as
taxation is in England, and as the decrees
concerning property are in the best regulated
courts of equity. This may appear very bold
after what has been said so often to the
contrary, by a gentleman once in full possession of the public confidence. That day,
however, is now gone by, and the people
reasoning by analogy, say, that he who can
artfully misrepresent the affairs of our near-
est neighbours, may be justly suspected of
misstating things that happened very remote both in time and place. The gentleman I allude to, in the brilliance of his
speeches, and the rhetorical exuberance of
his writings, is almost without an equal;

but

but in plain reafoning, in the clofe inveftigation of facts, in the accurate weighing
and balancing of merit and demerit, in making fair deductions and candid ftatements,
he is miferably deficient. There is nothing
which mankind ought to guard againft
more than what is called Oratory. It is to
the underftanding, what optical glaffes are to
the eye. The ufe of the former, like that
of the latter, is to magnify or diminifh the
apparent fize of objects.

The facts I have juft mentioned make
up the principal fum of criminality yet
brought forward againft Mr. Haftings; for
as to the fufpicion of his having intended to
apply the money he received for the Company, to his own ufe, I never can be perfuaded that it was of importance enough to
excite a parliamentary profecution.

Here I wifh the reader to paufe for a
few moments; and if he be converfant with

the

the hiftory of the world in general, or with
that of his own country in particular, to
afk himfelf this queftion : 'Can there be an
example found in the whole courfe of my
reading of a man fo feverely punifhed for
acts of fuch doubtful criminality ? Has
Mr. Haftings injured his country ? Has he
betrayed her intereft ? Has he by mifma-
nagement loft her provinces ? His greateft
enemies acquit him of all thefe things.
What is it, then, that they do lay to his
charge ? Why, they fay, that in his zeal to
defend the country committed to his care,
he taxed a zemindar, who his accufers
think ought not to have been taxed without
fome higher authority ; that he advifed the
Nabob of Oude to take from his unnatural
mother certain fums of money, his pater-
nal inheritance, of which fhe had defrauded
him. Thefe are the acts which are held
up to this country, now reaping the moft
folid and fubftantial benefits from them, as
crimes of the blackeft dye and of inexpiable

able guilt. Perhaps fome people who read this, will fufpect me of having taken the fame liberty in extenuating, as Mr. Haftings's accufers have done in aggravating his guilt. But this is not the cafe. In the Elucidation before alluded to, I gave all the arguments of his accufers their full weight; I abridged them of nothing but their harfh epithets. And here I hope I fhall be pardoned, if I hazard a fufpicion of my own, namely, that the length of the fpeeches, the profufion of epithets, the eccentric deviations from the fubject, and the rhetorical drefs of the accufations, were artfully intended to inflame the paffions, and bewilder the underftandings of the hearers. My reafon for thinking that confufion was ftudied more than elucidation, is this: I fcarcely ever converfed with any one man, who, though he had conftantly attended the trial, underftood the principal points which were at iffue between the accufers and accufed. The only things which feemed to imprefs

upon

upon the minds of the audience, were the strong terms of abuse, such as Captain General of Iniquity, Tyrant, Oppreſſor, Murderer, and ſo forth. Every one ſaid, that Mr. Haſtings muſt have done ſomething very bad, or ſuch epithets would not have been uſed.

The audience, who formed theſe haſty concluſions, did not recollect that the ſame voices which exclaimed againſt Mr. Haſtings, have in the very ſame manner, and in almoſt the very ſame words, exclaimed as loud againſt the Miniſters of this Country. Venality, Corruption, Ruin, and Impeachment, have been echoed and re-echoed in the chapel of St. Stephen, without producing any effect upon the people without doors. It may be aſked, why did the ſpeeches of the ſame men produce ſo much more effect againſt the miniſter of India, than againſt a miniſter of England? The reaſon is plain and obvious. In the latter

I

caſe,

cafe, the fcene of action was near and open
to the eye of every obferver ; the knowledge and experience of every individual
gave the lye to factious declamation, and
fictitious grievances. But in the former
cafe, the fcene of action was too remote,
both in time and place, for the people to
exercife their own judgment. They were
obliged to fee with the eyes of other men,
and take the accufations upon the credit of
the accufers : the voice of denial was borne
down by the charge of participancy of
guilt; ocular demonftration could not be
had in one cafe, as in the other ; add to this,
there is a natural propenfity in the human
mind to the believing of marvellous nar-
rations, which concern a remote period, or a
diftant country, and to the doubting of facts
which happened lately, or very near us.
Why this propenfity exifts in defiance of
reafon and common fenfe, I know not ; but
every one who examines the conduct of
mankind in all ages, muft fubfcribe to the
truth

truth of the obfervation. To raife a ftrong prefumption of guilt againft Mr. Haftings, his fortune was reprefented as enormoufly large. The firft idea that fprings up in the mind of every one upon hearing of large and rapid acquifitions, is, that the means were unjuftifiable. And we readily give a man, credit for the will, as foon as we are affured that he was poffeft of the power. For this reafon alone, the defence of a man accufed of peculation becomes extremely difficult. The object of accufation has to combat the natural prejudice of the mind. Experience fhows us, that by much the greater part of mankind are not proof againft temptation, and unlefs any individual has eftablifhed the moft unequivocal character for felf-denial, we are apt to fufpect, that he did not let flip any opportunity of improving his own circumftances. Some people, who are zealous fupporters of the dignity of human nature, may deny what I have now remarked; but if it be not true,

I cannot

I cannot account for the ready credit which is generally given to accufation, and denied to the affertions of innocence. I do not fay, that this preference is univerfal in all cafes, but I think the rule holds without an exception, when the accufation concerns thofe things to which men are naturally impelled by the force of paffions. Such, for example, are intrigues by young men for the poffeffion of women; and by men of a more advanced age for the poffeffion of wealth and power. I fhall not enter into a difcuffion of Mr. Haftings's fortune, nor of the means by which he acquired it. I fhall content myfelf with faying, that one of his former colleagues in office, and who muft be beft able to judge of the means, expreffes his wonder, not at the magnitude, but at the fmallnefs of Mr. Haftings's fortune, alledging, that his falary, properly managed, muft have accumulated a much larger fum than he is fuppofed to be poffeffed of.

We

We read lately in the public papers, of an officer of high rank in his Majefty's fervice, who had commanded armies in the fields of Indoftan, who was perfonally unacquainted with Mr. Haftings, delivering his fentiments of that gentleman; he faid, that the enemies of the Company in India bore the moft honourable teftimony to Mr. Haftings's ability, as a governor and a politician; that the people whom he was accufed of having oppreft, were extravagant in their praife of his juftice and moderation; that the country was more or lefs profperous and flourifhing, in proportion to the greater or lefs extent of Mr. Haftings's influence; that Bengal, which was immediately under his eye, was of all other provinces the moft happy and productive. But how, as we are told by the fame papers, was this evidence treated? *It was called an Arabian Night's Entertainment.* In the fame manner, the petitions of that very people, whofe fufferings are held up to the world as the

ground

ground of this impeachment, have been treated by the fame authority. The natives, inftead of praying for juftice againft Mr. Haftings, fupplicate juftice and mercy for him. They deny having fuffered under the government of Mr. Haftings; but how were their teftimonials and petitions an-ſwered? The late chief Manager told the Court, that thefe teftimonials fhould be among the firft evidence he would call to fupport his own allegations, and in proof of Mr. Haftings's oppreffion. The prefumption of innocence was fufpended by the curiofity which was excited in every one's mind, by the boldnefs of the promifed extraordinary conclufions; but the evidence of the teftimonials was never called for, and they were, or feem to be, wholly forgotten. I muft not omit one particular part of the fpeech which accompanied this promife, and which was, if poffible, ftill bolder than the promife itfelf.

The

The Court was defired to " confider thofe " who figned the teftimonials as people who " are forced to mix their praifes with their " groans, forced to fign with their hands " that had been in torture while yet warm " with thumbfcrews upon them, forced to " fign his praifes, and that, it was hoped, " would give their Lordfhips a full and fatis-" factory proof of the miferies of thefe poor " people." I think I may fafely affirm, that in all the annals of oratory, both ancient and modern, there never appeared a bolder figure, or a more extravagant hyperbole. Could the author of fuch words think fo meanly of his judges, as to flatter himfelf that fuch affertions, which carried, not improbability, but abfo-lute impoffibility on the face of them, could impofe upon their weaknefs and credulity? No, he knew better; but he hoped that it would keep alive the public clamour which was dying away with refpect to Mr. Haftings, and beginning to rife up againft himfelf.

He

He knew that Mr. Haftings had not the. fmalleft influence or controul over the natives of India; and that the very circumftance of the teftimonials having been tranfmitted home publicly by Lord Cornwallis, was an undeniable proof of their authenticity. Had there been a fufpicion of their having been obtained by compulfion, influence, or folicitation, it would have been an eafy matter to have inquired into the facts. There has been abundant time for doing as two years have elapfed fince they arrived in England. No attempt has been made to controvert their authenticity; and why? Becaufe no man, not even the chief manager himfelf, ever ferioufly doubted it. Upon this fubject I have but one thing more to remark, which is, that there never exifted an inftance previous to this, of profecuting a man for an injury, the perpetration of which was denied by thofe who alone had the means of knowing, and

I   affirmed

affirmed by thofe only who had not the means of knowing.

But the quotations I have already made, are but a fmall part of the contradictions which have arifen in the courfe of this impeachment. We find that the laft Houfe of Commons voted two refolutions perfectly in oppofition to each other, with refpect to the ftate of the province of Bengal. To criminate Mr. Haftings, and to make him appear as an oppreffive tyrant, Bengal was voted to be depopulated and ruined; to eftablifh the credit of the Eaft India Company, the fame country was voted to be rich, flourifhing, and productive. The laft Houfe of Commons was frequently reminded of thefe irreconcilable refolutions. Every member faw and felt it, but not one attempted to deny or juftify the fact: it was too plain for denial, and it was too grofs for juftification; the reproach was heard with confcious filence and affectation of contempt.

tempt. It was stated among other things in a newspaper, and the paragraph was construed into a libel upon the House of Commons. The author, whom the *mens conscia recti* had induced to affix his name to it, was punished; but upon what grounds? Not for publishing an untruth, but for violating the privilege of Parliament. Other offences of a similar nature, attended with more aggravating circumstances, had been committed by other men, and were passed over without punishment, and almost without notice. The member who had been thus treated, announced his intention of bringing forward a motion with respect to the contradictory resolutions above mentioned. A day was appointed, but before that day came, every engine was set to work to prevent its coming forward, or to render it abortive. He was prevailed upon to abandon the motion, for which he has been justly condemned both by his friends and enemies. The previous question might

have

have been moved to prevent the difcuffion, but the very fhrinking from examination would have eftablifhed the fact : but the fact cannot ftand in need of any eftablifh-ment, for any man by turning to the charges voted againft Mr. Haftings, and to the re-folutions of the Houfe of Commons upon the opening of the India budget, may con-vince himfelf of the truth of what has been afferted. The price of India ftock rofe two per cent. upon the credit given to the laft refolution, but I cannot fay that it fell upon the credit of the former. The ill confequence of abandoning the motion above mentioned is now felt, for we have heard this parliamentary cenfure made ufe of to prove that no fuch contradictions ex-ifted.

A country gentleman is faid to have urged thefe apparent contradictions in the votes of the laft Houfe of Commons con-cerning India, as the ground of his chan-

ging

ging his sentiments in regard to the merit of the impeachment. But how were these arguments treated? He was told that they had been *scouted* as often as they had been used by a gentleman who was ultimately punished for the publication of them. The word *scouting* brings to my recollection a commanding officer in India, who always made it a rule in controversy, to *scout* the argument he could not answer. This I take to be the case of the gentleman in question, who has courage enough to *scout*, but not to deny the truth of the arguments urged against him. Is it reasonable to suppose, that had the facts been untrue or misstated, not one person would think it worth his while to deny them? There is no man whose mode of reasoning I suspect so much, as that of the late chief Manager of the impeachment; and the grounds of my suspicion so peculiarly attached to him, are, that I scarcely ever read three pages of his writing, or heard him speak for ten minutes

E   at

at a time, without discovering some fallacy or other. The vast flow of words which he is master of, and the thick rich dresses which the wardrobe of his imagination can furnish at a moment's warning, enable him to conceal the greatest deformities, and to give falsehood and absurdity the appearance of truth and reason. I read his late pamphlet with the most jealous eye, and though my judgement was sometimes dazzled with the splendour of his diction on the first reading, I discovered a plentiful crop of false premises and unjust conclusions upon the second.

Having said thus much concerning the nature of the impeachment, as it stood in the last Parliament, chiefly for the sake of those who, not having read what I formerly wrote on that subject, may happen to peruse this, I shall now make some observations on the present stage of this flow and artfully embarrassed prosecution.

A ques-

A queſtion will ſoon be agitated, whether the proceedings ſhall be renewed or dif-
continued. The arguments in favour of
renovation or continuance are principally
theſe :

1. It muſt be for the advantage of Mr.
Haſtings that the trial ſhould proceed, becauſe, without an acquittal, his character
will deſcend to poſterity, not in ſuch fair
colours as it ought to do, if he be innocent.

2. That the preſent Houſe of Commons
is in honour, if not in law, bound by the
reſolutions of the laſt.

3. That to ſuffer crimes of notoriety and
enormity to eſcape without puniſhment,
would lower the dignity of the Britiſh
Parliament in the eyes of all Europe; and
in the opinions of the native princes and inhabitants of Indoſtan, it would amount to
a denial or failure of juſtice.

E 2   4. That

4. That Mr. Haftings's efcape by the diffolution of Parliament would prove an encouragement to future offenders to fpin out their trials by procraftination and delay, fo as to extend them beyond the life of one Parliament.

5. That to difcontinue the proceedings on account of paft delays, and the probability of future, would be to reflect on the conduct of the late Managers.

6. That ftrict juftice ought to be done, let the difficulties be ever fo many or fo great, and let the confequences be what they may : *Fiat juftitia, ruat coelum.*

Thefe are the principal reafons I have yet heard urged in favour of renovating or continuing the profecution. I fhall now examine them one by one in the order in which I have fet them down.

In regard to the firft, I readily agree that it would be for the intereft of Mr. Haftings that the trial fhould go on; but there are certain provifos requifite, without which it muft be an irreparable injury. Thefe provifos are, I fear, unattainable. The firft requifite is, that there fhould be a moral certainty, or, at leaft, a very ftrong probability of the trial's ending in the fpace of one Seffion of Parliament. This is, in its own nature, unattainable. It would derogate from the dignity of both Houfes, to enter into a compromife with a prifoner at the bar. It is alfo incompatible with the very nature of fupreme Courts of criminal juftice, to fix limitations to the number of charges, and to fet bounds to their own authority. The only poffible method of fhortening the duration of Impeachments, without infringing on the rights of one Houfe or the other, would be, by an exercife of the royal prerogative, to keep the Parliament fitting, without any prorogation, till the

trial

trial fhould be ended. But Mr. Haftings is not of confequence enough to expect fuch an exertion in his favour. He has no right to hope that all public bufinefs fhould be fufpended, and his cafe to be the only fubject of Parliamentary attention. The Lords have hitherto avoided fitting in Weft-minfter Hall during the fevereft part of the winter, for their health's fake; and in the fpring, which is the only feafon that has been devoted to this trial, they have not leifure to fit more than two or three days at fartheft, in a week. The experience of three years proves that twenty-three days, on an average, are the moft that can be given to Weftminfter Hall in one feffion; for in three years the Lords have fat juft fixty-nine days. Arguing from what has been to what muft be, we may fairly conclude, that more than the number above mention-ed cannot be allotted to this trial for the three years to come. In eftimating the pro-bable duration of the trial, I fhall not fol-

low

low the example of a gentleman, who made it appear that upon the prefent fyftem, it could not end in lefs than forty years.*

But I will take what I have heard for granted, namely, that the late Managers, if re-elected, would abandon all the remaining articles, except one, namely, that of contracts. We all faw that the laft charge, viz, that of prefents, occupied the fpace of two Seffions of Parliament in the profecution only. Now the charge of contracts is in its own nature capable of much more amplification than that of prefents. The latter divided itfelf into only two heads, that of avowed, and that

---

* This gentleman's calculation was founded upon falfe premifes. The true way of calculating the trial's duration by analogy, is this: the firft two charges were got through by the profecutors in one feffion; the next article has taken up two years, and we may reafonably allow the fame time for the next, which will make up four years for the fecond pair of articles. Here we difcover the ratio of increafing retar-

that of concealed prefents; but the former
will refolve itfelf into four heads, there being that number of contracts to be inquired
into. There will confequently be a much
wider field open for evidence and declama-

retardation, or which is the fame thing, the decreafe
of velocity. But we find the ratio to be in geometri-
cal progreffion, that is, every pair of articles requires
four times as many years to be got through, as their
immediate predeceffors did; this being fettled and the
rule eftablifhed, the calculation ftands thus: There
are twenty, or ten pair of articles in the whole.

1ft	Pair of Articles,	1	Year.
2d	Ditto —	— 4	Ditto.
3d	Ditto —	— 16	Ditto.
4th	Ditto —	— 64	Ditto.
5th	Ditto —	— 256	Ditto.
6th	Ditto —	— 1024	Ditto.
7th	Ditto —	— 4096	Ditto.
8th	Ditto —	16384	Ditto.
9th	Ditto —	65536	Ditto.
10th	Ditto —	262144	Ditto.
Total		349525	Years for the profe-cution only.

This may appear laughable, but I infift upon its
being the faireft calculation yet made, if we are to
reafon by analogy.

tion,

tion, as muft be evident to every one who confiders that it will be neceffary to examine the price of the articles contracted for, by way of afcertaining the profits of the contracts. It will lead alfo to an inquiry into the characters and refponfibility of the fuccefsful and difappointed candidates, in order to fhow why a preference was, or fhould have been given to the propofals of this man or the other. It will be neceffary alfo to trace the hiftory of former contracts, and to fhow the cuftoms and ufage of government in like cafes, and to compare the whole with the orders from the direction at home. A thoufand other difficulties will occur which I have not time to point out, nor the ability to forefee. Every one who has heard or read the fpeeches of the late chief Manager, and fome of his affociates, knows, that either of them can fpeak four or five days upon the moft trifling fubject. We are all certain of their powers, and what reafon have they ever given us to fufpect their inclinations ? Two years would not finifh the pro-

F   fecution

fecution upon this one article of contracts, even if the future Managers fhould be more œconomical of their oratory than their predeceffors. After this muft come the defence of four charges, which, on the defendant's fide, may take three or four years more, and this defence muft be followed by a replication, which will require a year or two more at leaft. Thefe eftimates taken together, amount to a greater length of time than Mr. Haftings can afford to fpend, from a life already fo far advanced, under the torture of hopelefs perfecutión.

Another provifo is alfo requifite to make it a defirable thing for Mr. Haftings that the trial fhould proceed; viz. that the accufers and accufed fhould be nearer upon a footing at the bar of the Houfe of Lords, than the Commons feem willing to admit. It is in vain for a Lord Chancellor or a High Steward, to tell the prifoner to be of good cheer, and not to fuffer depreffion from the weight of his accufers, if the defendants and profe-

cutors

cutors are not intitled to the fame indulgen-
ces from the Court. The very doctrine of
Lex et Confuetudo Parliamenti is fufficient
to difcourage any prifoner from placing
much confidence in his own defence. For
what is this *Lex et Confuetudo Parliamenti**
but a right claimed by the Commons to fettle their own privileges, 'not in a fixed and
invariable code made for general purpofes,
but according as occafions may arife ? The
judges would not take upon them to declare what were the privileges of Parliament,
but left each Houfe to fettle their own. But
even this power of fixing their own privileges would not be fo dangerous to the fubject, if they were fo fettled and reduced to

---

* The definition of this law and cuftom, accord-
to Vaughan, who was a ftrong advocate for it in the
the cafe of Lord Clarendon, is, *Lex ab omnibus quæ-
renda, à multis ignorata et à paucis cognita.* If for
paucis we read *nemine,* the definition is admirable.
But I apprehend that *paucis* fignifies the leaders of
the prevailing party in the Houfe of Comnons, and,
if fo, the true meaning of *Lex et Confuetudo Parliamenti* is, the privilege of making privileges.

writing

writing as to enable any man to say, Thus far Parliament may go and no farther. Unless the object of accusation could discover the *ne plus ultra* of the power of his accusers, the contest with such a body is like fencing without a foil, or fighting without a sword with an experienced gladiator. I believe there is no instance of an acquittal upon a Parliamentary impeachment, and if there is, I cannot call it to mind at this moment. There are many instances of impeachments inconsiderately undertaken and discontinued upon various pretexts, and some cases where impeachments have ended in bills of attainder. But if a prisoner were acquitted, the Commons may impeach again. Should any House of Commons ever consider it as derogatory to their dignity to be defeated by an individual, they may renew and persevere in their prosecutions till they have crushed him to atoms. Let the reader reflect for a moment on the inequality of the contest between the House of Commons and an Individual. Twenty Managers of select

abi-

abilities, aided by a number of common and civil lawyers, oppofed to a prifoner and three counfel. The former invefted with powers to call for what papers they pleafe, to fend for and examine what witneffes they think proper, and to make ufe of the public purfe for defraying the expences of the profecu-tion. The prifoner has none of thefe ad-vantages. I could enumerate many more on the fide of the profecutors; but they are fo obvious to every one that reflects, that it were a lofs of time to do it. It has been afked, what are Mr. Haftings's wifhes on this fubject, and why do not his friends come forward upon the occafion? In my opinion, it matters very little what he wifhes or defires. The votes of the Houfe of Commons ought not to be influenced by confiderations of this nature. Thofe mem-bers who think him guilty of fuch crimes as deferve everlafting punifhment, who think him deferving, not only what he has fuffered, but all that ingenuity can make him fuffer, will and ought to vote for the

renovation or continuance of the profecution. But thofe who think him guilty
of no crime, or that his paft fufferings have
more than expiated his offences, together
with thofe who think it incompatible with
the genius and fpirit of the Britifh laws,
that a man fhould be upon trial for his
whole life, will, doubtlefs, vote againft it. I
do not know what Mr. Haftings's wifhes
are upon this queftion ; I have heard him
fay, that no man fhould know his fentiments, a refolution wifely adopted, and
which he fhould have adopted four years
ago. After the Commons had loaded their
Journals with criminal allegations againft
him, he by his friends expreffed a wifh to
be impeached, in order that he might have
an opportunity of anfwering the accufation.
Little did he think at that time, that fo far
from obtaining the object of his wifhes, he
was fupplicating his own mifery and de-
ftruction. Let him, however, benefit from
experience, and take care how he becomes
acceffary to his own injuries.

I

With

With regard to the retrieval of character by acquittal, I can only fay that *vitæ fumma brevis, fpem nos vetat inchoare longam.* The profpect is too diftant for the moft fanguine hope, even if it were refolved to let him enter immediately on his defence. It would then be a work of three years, at the very loweft computation.

I know that fome people will fay, that I have over-rated the time, but I muft again appeal to experience as the foundation of probability. Let us recollect, that the late Managers fpent twenty days in making fine fpeeches, and eleven days in debating upon the admiffibility of evidence. The fubjects for dilatation will be more in number, and more ample in fubftance than thofe that have already occurred. So much time has elapfed fince the fpeeches were made, that the impreffions are nearly effaced, and will confequently require to be made anew. There will be all the characters of the defendants witneffes to be cut up, and their tefti-

mony

mony to be invalidated and explained away. The fpeeches of Mr. Haftings's counfel, which will doubtlefs be very long, muft be anfwered. A variety of circumftances will arife to occafion delay; circumftances which cannot be forefeen or prevented. As many or more, if the Managers are fo inclined, may be defignedly created. At the rate of twenty-three days for one feffion, all thefe things cannot be accomplifhed in lefs than three or four years. I am not confcious of having ufed any exaggeration, and I do defy any perfon to impeach the probability of my predictions or the juftice of my conclufions. It may be faid, for I have heard it faid, that the Houfe of Commons will take care that no fuch delays fhall happen in future. But great and powerful as that Houfe is; they are not equal to the tafk. When the late chief Manager and his colleagues are re-appointed, what power upon earth can put the bridle upon their tongues, or limit the length of their fpeeches ? There muft be in the conducting of ftate trials fo much

much left to the Managers, that they may protract and procraftinate juft. as much as they pleafe. There is no remedy but that of changing them, and that would amount to an annihilation of the proceedings, or at leaft to a difcontinuance of the fuit. The obfervations which the late chief Manager made upon the reproof given him by the then Houfe of Commons for charging Mr. Haftings with the death of Nundcomar, are frefh in the memories of all who heard him.

Under thefe circumftances, Mr. Haftings cannot wifh (at leaft I fhould think fo) for a renovation of the proceedings. In regard to his character, he muft leave it to the candour of pofterity, who having no perfonal refentment againft him, no danger to apprehend from his acquittal, may be inclined to think (what moft difinterefted people do at prefent) that the written teftimonials of the natives over whom he prefided, with refpect to his moderation and juftice, and the evidence

G   and

and admiffion of his enemies with refpect to his fervices, are a full refutation of oratorical abufe, and illiberal, ftudied invective. The character of his chief accufer, high as it may ftand for great talents and literary accomplifhments, will weigh not very heavy in the fcale of popular opinion, when oppofed to the plain affirmation of knowledge and integrity. It will be remembered, that he who contradicted the teftimonials of thoufands in favour of that governor general, whom they venerated and adored, had effrontery enough to contradict the oral teftimony of millions groaning under the oppreffion of an arbitrary government. It will be remembered, that he who raifed his voice to the utmoft pitch for the liberty of America, employed his proftituted pen for the enflaving of another kingdom. Biographers will publifh the hiftory and anecdotes of his life; and in comparing his orations and writings with each other, they will be ftruck with the glaring contradictions

tions and abſurdities of his various tenets
and opinions. Poſterity will ſee in his character little to commend, much to admire,
but infinitely more to lament and reprobate.
From the aſperſions of ſuch men there is
little to apprehend on account of future reputation. It is, however, a ſerious evil to
have ſuch a maſs of criminating matter,
wherein there is little intelligible, except
the terms of abuſe, left ſtanding againſt an
accuſed perſon on the Journals of the Lords,
without an anſwer or attempt at refutation.
But great as this evil may be, it is ſtill a
greater to be fixed to the bar for life, without a gleam of hope, or the moſt diſtant
proſpect of concluſion.

The next reaſon for continuance is,
that the preſent Houſe of Commons is in
honour, though not in law, bound by the
reſolutions of the laſt.

It

It may be eafy enough to make a pathetic fpeech upon this fubject, and to reprefent a diffolving Houfe of Commons in the charac-ter of a dying father conjuring and admonifh-ing his heirs to go on with a law, fuit which he himfelf had undertaken for fome capri-cious reafon or other. I am, however, much inclined to think, that as foon as the litigious father was interred, moft people would advife the heir to examine well the grounds of litigation, and unlefs there were more weighty reafons for continuing than abandoning the profecution, to let it drop immediately upon the father's death. I think no rational being would carry his ideas of filial obedience to the requeft of a dying father, fo far as to violate the firft precepts and injunctions of Chriftianity. But a com-parifon of this kind is no ways applicable to the cafe of a diffolved and a fucceeding par-liament. If the latter were bound in the fmalleft degree by the votes of the former, it would prevent the repeal of detrimental

ftatutes,

ftatutes,.. and the amendment of every error whatever. The laws of Great Britain would become like the laws of the Medes and Perfians,. fixed and unalterable. The doctrine is fo abfurd, that I would as foon fet about a ferious demonftration of the exiftence of light and darknefs, as undertake a refutation of fo palpable an abfurdity. I fhould fuppofe, that the gentleman I have often alluded to, in his wildeft and moft eccentric flights, would not maintain fo abfurd a propofition, as that a fucceeding Parliament is bound, either by honour or law, to accede to the votes of their predeceffors. Certainly the former ought to examine before they reject, in the fame manner as they fatisfy themfelves of the inexpediency of a ftatute before they repeal it. The laft Houfe of Commons are not entitled to an extraordinary degree of credit; for that they did vote contradictions, is clear beyond a doubt. The prefent Houfe, when the India minifter brings forward his budget, will, probably,

have

have their affent called for to fimilar propofitions. They will vote India to be in a
flourifhing ftate in the evening, and the
next morning they may go into Weftminfter Hall to tell the lords, that Mr. Haftings
has ruined the provinces of Bengal and Ba-
har beyond the power of reftoration. Many
fpecious arguments may be made ufe of to
entrap unwary members into a belief, that
having voted the exiftence or dependence of
an impeachment, they are bound by honour
and a juft regard to confiftency to go on with
it. But let it be remembered, that the right
and the expediency of enforcing that right,
are as diftinct as two propofitions can poffibly be from each other. In examining
the queftion of expediency, the Houfe will,
probably, recollect that the leaders of the
two parties, which then generally oppofed
each other, were divided in their opinions
with refpect to the points of criminality.
Both agreed there was fomething criminal,
but what that fomething was, they could

not

not settle among themselves. It was urged
as a reason why the abstract question of
abatement or dependence of an impeachment
on a dissolution of Parliament, should be dis-
cussed separately and without reference to the
particular case which gave rise to the question, that if that disjunctive mode were not
adopted, it would be impossible for posterity
to know upon what basis the resolution was
founded. The votes of some might be influenced by one consideration, and some by
another. Some might vote against farther
discussion from despair of ever seeing the
trial ended. Others from humanity to-
wards the prisoner; and others, because in
their opinions a dissolution of Parliament ex-
tinguished an impeachment. These arguments had deservedly much weight; but it
is to be lamented, that the same objections
had not been made to that sweeping vote,
which passed upon the Benares article; for
in that instance, though a majority of
thirty-nine agreed that there was something
criminal

criminal in one allegation or another, yet, had the allegations been difcuffed feparately, there would not have been a majority in favour of criminality in any one point or allegation in the whole article. There is fcarcely a man living whofe conduct, even for one day, would bear fuch a fcrutiny as Mr. Haftings's has undergone in this impeachment. You will fcarcely ever find a perfon who does not difcover fomething wrong in every tranfaction which he analizes and examines. Suppofe the minifter on a late occafion had been compelled to lay before the public the whole procefs of the convention; has any perfon a doubt but that the ingenuity of his enemies would have difcovered fomething really or apparently reprehenfible in his conduct? I believe it is a maxim that admits of no difpute, that no minifter can hold his fituation in this country longer than he can keep a majority to fupport him in both Houfes; and I think it is equally clear, that no minifter

nifter

nifter would keep that majority long, if he were obliged to expofe every tranfaction, with all its concomitant *minutiæ*, to public inveftigation. The reafon of this is, that let a Minifter's conduct be as intentionally pure as the fnow upon the mountains, it would be eafy for thofe who envy his fitu-ation, to give his actions fuch a colour and hue, as muft unavoidably render him unpo-pular, and confequently drive him from his place. When I confider how the enemies of Mr. Haftings have had accefs to all his public and much of his private correfpon-dence, how they have ranfacked every fe-cret abyfs and corner for matter to bring againft him, it is really a miracle that they have not been able to find fomething better to lay hold of, than any thing they have yet urged againft him.

The reafons which I have already ftated, are fufficient of themfelves, but I could bring many more, why the prefent Houfe

of Commons, before they determine to re-
commence the profecution, fhould accu-
rately examine every article and allegation.
If they haftily adopt them as their own, the
chief Manager may at a future period tell
them, as he did their predeceffors, that the
impeachment was as much theirs as his.
He might confider them as anfwerable
for every miftake that had crept into the
articles. And, doubtlefs, they would be fo
in fair and true conftruction. It would be
founded forth to the world, that the adoption of the articles by the prefent Houfe of
Commons was an undeniable proof of their
truth and importance. It would be ufed as
an argument againft the prifoner in one
Houfe, and very poffibly at fome future
time againft thofe who adopted the refolutions in another. It is very reafonable to
expect, that thofe who took an active part in
bringing this impeachment forward, will
ufe every argument, however fallacious, to
prevail with the prefent Houfe to give it
their

their unqualified approbation and adoption. But furely it is quite the reverfe with refpect to the new members, and to thofe who either voted againft it, or took no active concern in its fuccefs; it would be not only an act of injuftice to Mr. Haftings to adopt the trial without examination, but a breach of that duty which every reprefentative owes to his conftituents. The great ufe of changing our reprefentatives, is to give the people an opportunity of rejudging their deputies, and of correcting the errors of their old reprefetatives, by fubjecting their acts to the revifal and judgment of their new.

The third reafon for the continuance of the impeachment is, that if crimes of fuch notoriety and enormity are fuffered to efcape unpunifhed, it would lower the dignity of the Britifh Parliament in the eyes of all Europe; and in the opinions of the princes and natives of Indoftan, it would amount to a denial or failure of juftice.

With

With refpect to the diminution of dignity in the eyes of all Europe, I have this to remark, that were a queftion ftated abftractly, can it become the dignity of an individual, of a body corporate, or of any affembly of people whatever, to carry on a criminal profecution againft one man, for the fame crime for feven years or longer? I think there could be but one anfwer given to it.

Were another queftion ftated in the fame abftract way, does it become the dignity of a Prince, of a Miniftry, of a Parliament, or of any ruling body, to employ a fervant in a high ftation, neceffarily invefted with many difcretionary powers for a great number of years, and after he has refigned his office, to bring him to trial for actions which his fuperiors had been informed of regularly, and which had received the avowed approbation of fome of his fuperiors, and the tacit implied approbation of all? I think there could not be two anfwers given to

this

this queſtion. How then is it poſſible that the dignity of Parliament can ſuffer by the abandoning of ſuch a proſecution. But it muſt reflect upon the wiſdom of our anceſtors in the eyes of all the world, when it is conſidered, that it is not repugnant to any written law which they have eſtabliſhed, for a man to be kept upon his trial for one and the ſame offence for his whole life. It is ſeldom that laws are enacted in any ſtate till occaſion calls for them. Our anceſtors ſaw many oppreſſions by the crown, and they guarded againſt them, but there never exiſted an inſtance before the preſent one of cruſhing a man by the bulk, not by the ſpecific weight of accuſation. For this reaſon they made no ſtatute of limitations with regard to Parliamentary impeachments, but ſurely now the evil does exiſt, it calls aloud for remedy and redreſs. Our Parliamentary anceſtors acquired infinite honour to themſelves, and conferred an ineſtimable obligation upon their grateful poſterity, by their

their fuccefsful ftruggles in favour of liberty againft the defpotifm and tyranny of Kings; and our cotemporary legiflators would acquire equal honour to themfelves, and confer equal benefit upon us and our pofterity, if they would frame fuch a ftatute or law, as would prevent themfelves or their fucceffors from carrying their refentment' and vengeance beyond the bounds of reafon and juftice.

With refpect to the opinions of the princes and inhabitants of India, I would advife thofe who think that the honour of Parliament would fuffer in their eyes, if Mr. Haftings's perfecution were dropped, to recollect the teftimonials which thefe princes and inhabitants fent over in his favour about two years ago. I would then afk the fupporters of this argument, whether this nation would think it derogatory to the honour of his Majefty, were he to grant a pardon to a prifoner under fentence of death, in confequence of a

peti-

petition figned by many thoufands of his
moft refpectable fubjects? But the cafe of
Mr. Haftings is much ftronger, for the natives of India do not afk a pardon for him
for offences committed, but they fay he has
done nothing to make him ftand in need of
it. In order to enter in the opinions of
other men, we muft reduce our own
knowledge down to the ftandard of theirs,
or raife them to the fame level: we
muft take up their prejudices in favour of
their own laws and cuftoms : in fhort, we
muft place ourfelves as nearly as poffible in
their fituations. To exemplify this, let the
reader fuppofe himfelf one of the India
Princes or Zemindars who figned the teftimonials ; he is told, that after Mr. Haftings
had quitted his government, he is impeached
for cruelty and oppreffion committed in India. Confcious of the falfehood of the accufation, and knowing that Mr. Haftings's
adminiftration, when compared with any
other he had ever feen, was lenient in the
extreme, he figns a teftimonial of his good

con-

conduct and petitions in his favour. Afterwards this Indian Prince is told, that his testimonial was not attended to, that those who could know nothing of the matter, were believed in preference to those who alone could know any thing about it. Suppose farther, that this Indian Prince should hereafter be told, that this governor, whom all India loved and adored, was kept upon his trial for eight or ten years, and lastly died from anxiety and despair. What ideas must he entertain of English laws and English justice? With such a view of our boasted constitution, (and this is the only view an Indian can take of it) would he not prefer the speedy sentence of Nader Shaw, to the lingering justice of a British legislature? What must a Mahommedan Cazy or Mufti think of our doctrine of evidence, when he compares it with their own? In their courts of justice, the strongest proofs are requisite to establish criminality, but when the Cazy is told, that with us a man may be convicted

of

of oppreffion upon the evidence of thofe who neither faw nor felt, in defiance of the teftimony of thofe who muft have feen and felt, had the oppreffions been committed; can he fail of treating our doctrine of evidence with contempt and abhorrence? I do not fay that fuch is the doctrine of evidence among us, in all cafes; but with the knowledge which the Indians poffefs, and from the premifes which are before them, they can make no other conclufions.

What can we reafon from, but what we know?
Pope's Effay on Man.

The fpirit of the Mahommedan laws, both ecclefiaftical and civil, is that of lenity. Captives taken in war are always faved by converfion to the faith, and murder itfelf is not punifhed with death, even in a flave, if the heirs will accept, and his mafter pay the ftipulated fine.* What opinions, then, muft the Mahommedans entertain of our laws, when thofe who are fup-

* Vid. Hedaga, a Mahommedan law book, tranflated by Mr. Hamilton, and now in the prefs.

I   pofed

pofed to have been injured, are not only prevented from remiffion of the injuries, but are not fuffered to bear teftimony in favour of the accufed, that no fuch injuries were done to them? Such ideas, as I have defcribed, the natives of India now entertain of this profecution. I have heard gentlemen who have lately returned from that country declare, that none of the Indians believe that Mr. Haftings is really profecuted on account of any thing he did in India : they fay, it may ferve as a pretext, but the real caufe muft be very different from the oftenfible one. In that opinion they are not fingular; for I have heard many people throw out fufpicions very unfavorable to the moral characters of fome of his accufers. They fay, that the *amor juftitiæ* never exaggerates, that the man who really loves and feeks juftice, will endeavour to convince the judgment, not to inflame the paffions; he will take care whilft he is doing juftice to one perfon, not to do an act of ftill greater injuftice to another. I think I

have

have sufficiently shewn, that it will be no diminution of honour to the present House of Commons, in the eyes of neighbouring states, nor in the opinions of the princes of India, if this prosecution be discontinued; on the contrary, I have proved, that the long duration of this trial has brought into view an imperfection in the Constitution, which has, till now, remained undiscovered.

We all understand the meaning of the words *honour* and *dignity*, but we are not all agreed, where to place them. In my opinion *true honour* and *dignity* consist in solid and substantial justice, and as there can be no justice in crushing an individual by a long and indefinite prosecution, so there can be neither honour nor dignity in doing it. I know it will be said, that it is disgraceful to Parliament to be baffled by an individual in their pursuit of justice. The proposition is true; but the present case does not

come

come within it. If the articles were inju-
dicioufly drawn; if they comprehended a
great deal of irrelevant matter; if they in-
cluded all the acts of a long adminiftration;
if they were from their unweildy and un-
manageable bulk, from their want of fhape
and form, totally unfit for a court of juftice, who are the parties to blame in this
tranfaction? Surely Mr. Haftings cannot
be blamed for things in which he had no
concern. The articles were drawn by a
Committee, and no doubt the late chief
Manager had a principal fhare. If we por-
tion out the particular fhares of blame, they
will be divided in this way. The gentleman juft alluded to was very injudicious,
and fhewed vaft want of technical fkill in
his profeffion, in framing fuch unweildy
articles. The Committee fhewed want of
judgment or of attention in not correcting
the errors of their chairman. And the late
Houfe of Commons paid too high a compliment to their Committee, when they
voted

voted the articles without more examination. Thefe are errors no ways imputable to Mr. Haftings. But that they are errors, and very grievous ones, no man will take upon him to deny. Here I would afk the moft zealous advocate for continuing the impeachment, whether there be either honour, dignity, juftice, or any thing laudable in perfevering in error and miftake. I know that every argument will be urged that ingenuity can invent, to make the prefent Houfe of Commons believe that their honour is committed ; and the true caufe of making this attempt is, that the articles cannot be abandoned without an implied reflection upon him that framed them. But the queftions for the confideration of every member are thefe : Shall we prefer juftice to injuftice ? Or fhall we facrifice our own honour to fave that of another man ?

The fourth reafon for continuing the impeachment is, that if Mr. Haftings be fuffered

fered to escape by diffolution of Parliament, it will encourage other offenders to use the arts of delay, and to defeat justice by protracting the trial beyond the life of one Parliament.

This objection to discontinuance has no weight, for the Commons may renovate process if they think fit. Besides, no one can impute delay to Mr. Haftings. It has been said, in answer to the complaints made by his friends on the score of delay, that he might have defended himself article by article, and that it was the wish of the Managers that he should do so.

A proposal of that kind never would have been made, had not the Managers seen in it great advantages to themselves. They would have had the advantage of turning the admissions in his defence upon the first article into evidence to criminate him upon the next. It may be said, that actions really inno-

innocent cannot be tortured into criminality ; and that a man ought in ſtrict juſtice to be puniſhed for crimes, let them be brought to light how they may. This is undeniably true when applied to crimes that are in their own nature criminal, and perhaps it may hold good, when applied to poſitive or prohibited crimes ; but by no means when applied to *ex poſt faɛto* criminality, ſuch as the taxing of a zemindar, who in the opinion of ſome was not taxable. But all the crimes imputed to Mr. Haſtings are of that nature. They are merely ſpeculative; ſuch for example, was his receiving money for the uſe of the Company, under an idea that the law ſanctioned it. To make the very worſt of that offence, it amounts to no more than an involuntary miſtake, which cannot be claſſed among the *mala in ſe*, nor the *mala prohibita*. When miſtakes, not only perfectly innocent, but highly beneficial to his country, are tortured into acts of inexpiable criminality, ſurely the

ac-

accufed is juftified in withholding from his accufers all the information he can. Notwithftanding thefe unfair advantages taken againft him, Mr. Haftings, of himfelf, would not have objected to the mode of trial propofed by his accufers. The objection was made by his counfel, who, in contending for the prefent mode, acted as all other profeffional men would, that is, infifted upon that which the law allowed them, and they thought moft advantageous to themfelves in conducting the defence. It was lately urged as an argument in favour of proceeding with the old articles, rather than to begin *de novo*, that it would be an injuftice to the accufed, for the profecutors to avail themfelves of his defence, in the conftructing of new charges. But the great evil which would have lighted upon Mr. Haftings, had the mode of trial propofed by the Managers been acceded to or decided in their favour, is this; he would from that moment have been certain of being condemned,

or

or he muft have fought through the whole twenty articles. For had he been acquitted upon nineteen, they would have tried the twentieth. One of the Managers, who is well verfed in the doctrine of chances, and who was the propofer, if not the contriver, of this new mode of trial, knows very well, that if the chances upon any one or every one of the articles taken feparately, were nineteen to one in the prifoner's favour, there would be almoft a certainty of convicting him upon one or the other of the twenty. He knew very well, that no man either in public or private life can conduct himfelf without fome faults, and he knew alfo that there was nothing fo white but himfelf and his colleagues could tinge it with black.

It is impoffible for the ingenuity of man to charge Mr. Haftings with delay, or being the caufe of delay.

K   The

The fifth objection I have heard to discontinuance, is, that to abandon the profecution upon account of the paft delay and probable future, would reflect upon the conduct of the late Managers.

I have fhown already, that more refpect is due to fubftantial juftice, than to the character of any individual whatfoever, and I could make it evidently appear, if it were neceffary, that the refolutions of the laft Houfe of Commons, though moved by the chief Manager himfelf, did bear very hard upon his own character. For what was the purport of them? It was to enable the Managers to lay down a load which their own indifcretion had laid upon their own fhoulders. It was a tacit acknowledgement that they had overloaded the articles.* To blind

---

* If any other man had done this, the chief manager would have compared him to the voracious glutton difcharging the fuperfluous crudities of an overloaded ftomach.

the

the eyes of the public, and to cover their
own errors, they talked about the avocations
of the judges; but they muft have been
very ignorant indeed, if they did not know
that the judges muft devote part of their
time to their other duties. When circumftances arife, which no human fagacity can
forefee or guard againft, there is fome excufe for mifcarriage and failure of fuccefs,
but when all the impediments are obvious
and irremovable, there can be no excufe
pleaded for undertaking what cannot be per-
formed. The wifdom of thofe who drew
the articles, may be compared to that of a
man who begins to erect a palace, with not
money enough to build a cottage. It is
true, the chief Manager in his late pamphlet, ridicules reafon and calculation; but I
cannot help thinking that calculation, had
he condefcended to accept its affiftance,
would have been of great ufe to him in
drawing the articles in this impeachment.
It would have faved him from a difgrace,

K 2   which

which it is not in the power of this House
of Commons to wipe away from him, whether they adopt his articles or not. His mif-
conduct may be of this use; it may prove
an useful leffon to future Parliaments to employ in ferious undertakings men of judgment, inftead of men of fancy and imagination. I hope I fhall not incur the difplea-
fure of the prefent Houfe of Commons,
when I fay that their predeceffors proclaim-
ed to the world their own errors, when they
determined to abandon fixteen parts out of
twenty of their accufations; and they pro-
claimed their own injuftice, when in the
very act of abandoning them, they infifted
upon their truth and importance. The chief
Manager muft have felt himfelf very un-
comfortable, when he made the motion for
abandonment. He expofed himfelf to a
very juft rebuke, had any member thought
fit to give it to him. He might have been
thus addreffed : " You have perfuaded us to
" vote twenty articles ; you affured us you
" would

" would fubftantiate them all; you drew
" them yourfelf, and you had the aid of
" what counfel you thought fit to afk for and
" to confult. We placed our confidence in
" you and your affociates ; you have wafted
" our time in voting the articles which you
" now want to abandon ; you have put the
" prifoner to a vaft deal of unneceffary trou-
" ble and expence in anfwering them, and
" you now come to tell us, that we have
" voted more articles than can ever be
" tried in the life of man. The excufe
" you make, is, that the judges muft de-
" vote fome of the time to the courts
" of Weftminfter, and they muft go their
" circuits. All this you knew before."
Had any member made thefe obfervations,
I fee but one way of anfwering them, namely, by ribaldry, a method which the gentleman I allude to, always ufes as a fubftitute
for reafon, when reafon will not anfwer his
purpofe.

It

It has been faid, that the late chief Manager is as much upon his trial as Mr. Haftings. If this means his character only, I admit it; but I do not fee how his character is more concerned than that of every other leader of a parliamentary Impeachment. All impeachments are planned, contrived, and brought forward by a few, but they are adopted by the many. In the prefent cafe the members of both fides of the Houfe pinned their faith on the fleeves of their leaders, viz. the minifterial members on the minifter, and the oppofition members on the chief Manager. The latter in conducting the profecution committed his own honor and veracity more than was neceffary. He went out of his way to do it. The ftory of Deby Sing was not in the articles. It was not in the votes of the Commons: it was not in their inftructions. I never yet heard the warmeft advocate for the gentleman in queftion, attempt to defend his conduct in this bufinefs. It has been confidered by every

body,

body, as contrary to the principles of juftice to blacken the charaster of the accufed, with fudden and unexpeseted charges, to-tally foreign to the point of iffue, even if they were true. But there was a fallacy and a deception made ufe of in the ftatement, which can never be too often or too much expofed. The gentleman " would not have " believed it, had it not been upon the Com-" pany's records." The idea which public cords imprefs on an Englifh mind is, that a fuit has been tried, and is recorded. But what was upon the Company's records? Nothing more than that Mr. Paterfon had collested a number of *ex parte* complaints from the infurgents at Rungpore, and tranf-mitted them to the Board at Calcutta, and thence they were fent home. The truth of thefe complaints had never been inquired into, and were no more proved, than an in-distment for an affault can be faid to be proved, the moment the clerk has filled up the blanks in order to prefent the bill to the

grand

grand jury. The papers collected by Mr.
Paterfon were no more matters of record
than bills of indictment are before the grand
jury has feen them; this the chief Manager
knew very well, but he gave them the authenticity of records. The ftory of Deby
Sing is the grand point upon which the
gentleman's character for veracity is ftaked;
and this never can come to a decifion by
the Lords without a new charge voted by
the Commons. It is therefore evident, that
to continue the trial for the fake of knowing whether a great orator be a calumnia-
tor, is of no ufe, fince if the object were of
much greater importance, it is unattainable.

The fixth reafon I have heard urged for
continuing the trial is, that fubftantial juftice ought to be done, let the difficulties be
ever fo many or fo great, and the confequences what they will. *Fiat Juftitia, ruat
Cœlum*

Cælum. To this propofition I agree: but then the prefent Houfe of Commons ought to be well affured that there is a *dignus Vindice nodus.* The offences ought to be of that ferious nature, of that dangerous tendency, and alarming appearance, as may juftify the refentment and vindication of fuch a powerful body as the Houfe of Commons. Great bodies move flow, and it is very fit they fhould do fo; for wherever they fall, they fall heavy. In reading the hiftory of ftate profecutions, we are often fhocked at the violence of the times, and condemn the miftaken zeal of the accufers. Pofterity are always the beft judges of the merit and demerit of impeachments. When party confiderations ceafe to blind the eye of reafon, nothing is received into the fcale, but the evidence and internal criminality of facts. For this reafon every member, if he values his future reputation, if he wifhes to be thought hereafter the advocate of juftice rather than the fupporter of a party, will

L   from

from regard to himfelf, examine well the grounds upon which he affents to the prefent profecution. It is abfurd in the extreme, as I have fully demonftrated already, in the prefent Houfe of Commons to pay a compliment to the laft at the expence of their own honour and reputation. The very refolution to abandon four fifths of the articles was an unequivocal proof of the want of caution in the laft Houfe ; for it is impoffible for the chief Manager, with all his fubtlety to maintain, that they could be both *wifely* taken up and *wifely* laid down. He might as well attempt to bring the two poles together, as to reconcile two fuch oppofite conclufions. This alone, independent of the contradictory votes refpecting Bengal, and the numerous teftimonials in Mr. Haftings's favour, would be fufficient to juftify the prefent Houfe of Commons in refufing their hafty and unqualified affent to the refolutions of the laft. In his endeavour to gain fome, the late chief Manager will, doubt-

doubtleſs, endeavour to touch the feelings of many. He will exclaim againſt the inconſiſtency of thoſe who formerly voted for, and now vote againſt the impeachment. He may talk of turncoats, tergiverſation, and various other terms, according as his ſportive imagination may ſuggeſt them. But there is to be found in the laſt page of his Reflections on the Revolution in France, and in the very laſt ſentence of that page, a full juſtification of changed opinion : " *When* " *the equipoiſe of the veſſel is endangered by* " *overloading it upon one ſide, it is expedient to* " *carry the weight of reaſon to that which may* " *preſerve its equipoiſe.*" Many members who were formerly perſuaded to think Mr. Haſtings guilty, might with great propriety vote for the proſecution ; but they did not intend to vote for a perſecution, and I believe every one will agree, that a three years proſecution is a perſecution, and has all the effects of it. A proſecution becomes a perſecution whenever it is carried to ſuch a

length,

length, that if the object of accufation is found innocent, it is not in the power of any earthly being to make him compenfation. The prefent cafe falls within that defcription.

There is no inconfiftency in departing from the paths of error, nor in withdrawing an abufed confidence. ، Gentlemen, when called upon for their votes and opinions, muft give them upon that information which they have before them ; but if upon farther examination they find themfelves deceived, they would furely be blameable in the higheft degree for fhutting their eyes againft the light of conviction, and perfevering in what they know to be wrong. The doctrine of confiftency, if confiftency means perfevering in opinion whether right or wrong, would lead to numberlefs evil confequences, were it generally adopted. Many commoners, who made part of that Houfe, which voted the impeachment, are now

Peers,

Peers, and if they ſtudy confiſtency of opinion, rather than impartial juſtice, they muſt condemn the accuſed at all events. But one would think that a charge of in-confiſtency would become no man ſo ill as that gentleman, who of all others is the moſt likely to make it. I ſay, the moſt likely, becauſe it is his intereſt to do ſo. The inconfiſtencies of his political opinions were ſufficient to fill a pamphlet many years ago, and if collected up to the preſent time, would fill a folio. Notwithſtanding this, he will be the foremoſt to brand cor-rected error with the marks of levity and inconfiſtence. His motives are as obvious as they are cogent. It is impoſſible for any man to vote againſt continuing the im-peachment without a tacit condemnation of the chief conductor of it. He anticipates the ſentence, well knowing that it will ope-rate againſt him in the opinion of the world, as much as an acquittal of the priſoner by the lords. It will affect him ſtill more;

for

for as it will be more honourable for Mr.
Haftings to be acquitted by his profecutors
than by his judges, fo it will be more diſho-
nourable for the chief Manager to be abandoned by the Commons, than to be repulſed
by the Lords. I know there are thoſe who
contend that a dereliction of the trial by the
Commons would not clear the character of
Mr. Haftings ſo much as an acquittal by
the Lords. But the caſe is otherwiſe;
ſuppoſe him acquitted of the three articles
already brought forward, his enemies may
ſay, there are ſeventeen more, all criminal
in the eyes of the laſt Houſe of Commons,
and dropt, not from confideration of pro-
bable innocence, but of certain inconve-
nience in profecuting them. His friends in
anſwer can only reaſon from analogy.
They may ſay, that the Managers tried
him upon thoſe charges which to them
appeared moſt likely to convict him.
This may be anſwered again; the Commons in a former impeachment (that of
Lord

Lord Oxford) inverted the rule, and chofe to try mifdemeanours before treafons, and we have therefore a right to fuppofe in this inftance, that they began with charges of the leaft criminality. An acquittal by the Commons would cure all this, and the innocence of the accufed would reft, not upon likelihood and probability, but upon the altered opinions of his accufers.

If I am not much deceived, I have in the foregoing pages demonftrated, that none of the reafons hitherto urged for continuing the impeachment without an attentive re-examination of the articles, have any real weight in them. It cannot be a defirable thing to the prifoner, in any fhape ; for fuppofing him fure of being acquitted of the three or four articles, an acquittal of four cannot amount to an acquittal of twenty. But I have fhewn, that if the trial commences again, there is not a profpect of its being ended, except by death, during the

exif-

exiftence of this Parliament. Who can fet
bounds to the length of fpeeches, or to the
debates upon evidence? There is that kind
of equality between the two. Houfes, which
prevents the Lords from curbing the Managers, as the King's Bench may do, when the
Crown lawyers take too great liberties. It
is true, I have heard it faid, and with much
appearance of reafon, that the Managers are
at the bar of the Lords what the King's At-
torney General is at the bar of the King's
Bench, and intitled to no more authority and
refpect. This, however, does not agree with
the claims of the Managers, who contend
that they are clad with the robes of magif-
tracy, not in the gown of folicitation. It is
faid, alfo, that if a prifoner be acquitted, the
Commons' may impeach him again upon
the fame points of criminality. Now it is
not ufual to try a man twice upon the fame
indictment at the fuit of the King. With
fuch vaft difadvantages, it is a moft dreadful
thing

thing to enter into conteft with fo powerful a body.

I have fhewn, that fo far from its being derogatory to the honour and dignity of the Houfe of Commons, that it is a duty incumbent upon them to examine the conduct of their predeceffors in this profecution ; that though the laft Houfe joined iffue with the prifoner upon the plea of *guilty* or *not guilty*, the prefent Houfe has not yet gone that length ; that, to adopt the articles without due examination, would be an injuftice to the prifoner, and a breach of duty to the people ; for I think I am juftified in faying, that the profecution of Mr. Haftings is very unpopular. The people are not infenfible of his fervices, nor ungrateful ; for how can they doubt of his fervices, when the acting India Minifter has been heard to fay, that if Mr. Haftings would have accepted a qualified approbation, or a fet-off of merit againft

M de-

demerit, he would not have been impeached. The people were for a time misled by delusive oratory and declamation, but the mist of false accusation is dissipated.* They are convinced that it is the man, and not his

mea-

---

* It is curious to observe, that the two Republics Athens and Sparta, which disagreed in most other things, agreed perfectly in this proposition; namely, that Oratory without restraint was an insufferable evil. The former made a law to curb it, and the latter exploded the orator altogether. They both considered all aggravation as a downright lie. Other States in Greece entertained the same opinion of oratory; and permitted no orator to have a share in the administration of public affairs, until his moral character had undergone an examination: and it was also lawful for any citizen to prosecute an impostor, who had found means to conceal his vices from the knowledge of the inspectors. The Spartans had a vast antipathy to long speeches; for when an orator was endeavouring to speak the whole day on various subjects, they drove him out of the city. There was another thing well worth notice in Athenian jurisprudence; The Areopagus sate only in the night, and without light; a regulation, intended to prevent the judges from being prejudiced for or against

the

meafures, that have excited the indignation of his enemies. Who can think otherwife, when it is recollected that the very fyftem of politics, which was defended the other day fo ably in this Parliament, was as much reprobated in the laft but one ; I mean the fcheme for uniting the Indian princes, to crufh or reduce the power of that mercilefs tyrant, Tippoo Sultan. In Mr. Haftings this was a crime, in Lord Cornwallis it is a vir-

the accufed. The fame court made it a rule to confine the pleader to a fimple ftatement of facts, and allowed him to make no appeal to the paffions, in order to warp the judgment. This court of juftice was in the eftimation of Cicero, (than whom no man better underftood the ufe, and abufe of criminal judicature) fo effential to the conftitution of the republic, that he gave it as his opinion, that the univerfe might be as well conducted without the hand of Providence, as the government of Athens to exift without the Areopagus.

Vid. Mr. Mitford's Hiftory of Greece, &c.; and le Voyage du jeune Anacharfis, by Monfieur Barthelemi.

tue;

tue ; the changing of the whole revenue fyftem in Mr. Haftings was a crime, the pur-
fuing of the fame fyftem in Lord Cornwallis
a merit. Of this nature are all the accufations I have yet feen brought againft him.
The people begin to fee, or I fhould rather
fay, have feen for fome time, that his enemies are determined to torture, whom they
cannot deftroy; that if they cannot condemn him by the fentence, they will ruin
him by the delays of the law. I never met
among Mr. Haftings's greateft enemies
without doors, one man who did not reprobate the mode in which he has been profecuted. What ufe will it be to acquit a prifoner, when you have ruined his fortune,
broke his conftitution, and brought him to
the brink of the grave ? It never can be for
the honour and dignity of a Houfe of Commons to carry their vengeance againft an
individual, who has never injured them, nor
his country, to fuch a length as this has
been

been carried. Take his crimes for granted, nay, admit all the aggravations of his bittereft and moft implacable enemies to be literally true, the punifhment is greater than the offence; the Houfe of Commons fhould remember, that the power with which they are intrufted by the people of England, ought no more to be abufed, than the power intrufted to the Crown. The laws now in being have no provifion againft everlafting impeachment by the Commons; but if frequent inftances of this kind occur, the people may be neceffitated to fet limits to the privileges of their reprefentatives, as well as to the prerogatives of their Kings.* What avail Magna Charta and the Habeas Corpus act, if the ufe of them may be defeated by a new fpecies of profecution?

---

* It was a remark of Solon, that the moft perfect government is that, where an injury to one man is the concern of all.

I have

I have fhewn, alfo, in the courfe of this work, that the continuance of the impeachment muft diminifh the admiration which has hitherto been paid to our Conftitution by foreign nations, and that fo far from raifing the dignity of the Britifh Parliament in the eyes of Afiatic princes, it muft humble it in the extreme. The fpirit of divination will bufy itfelf in difcovering the real grounds of the profecution. They will take a retrofpective view of Mr. Haftings's adminiftration, and they will fay to themfelves, " his " profecution cannot originate from the wars " which he conducted, for in *them* he was " fuccefsful; it cannot originate in the re- " venue, for *that* he has improved; it cannot " originate from the fines which he levied on " apoftacy and rebellion, for *they* were ap- " plied to the fervice of the ftate; it cannot " originate in the acts of government, for he " has never tranfgreffed the laws and ufage of " the country. They will then turn their

I   eyes

eyes to the examples which have happened in their own times, and before their own eyes. They will recollect the instances of Jaffier Khan, and other delegated tyrants, whose extortions and oppressions filling the royal coffers, laid the foundation of their advancement, in rank and favour; and having never seen an instance of an oppressor being punished for oppression committed for the benefit of the sovereign, they will ultimately arrive at this conclusion; namely, that their late Governor General is prosecuted, not for what he did do, but for what he did not do; not for having extorted too much, but for not having extorted more. This conclusion, and the only one which they can draw from the premises before them, will naturally excite dread and horror of the British government. They will expect that future Governors, taking example from the sufferings of Mr. Hastings, will redouble their exertions to accumulate for

the

the fovereign, and to plunder the fubject.

But the dignity of the laft Houfe of Commons muft fuffer, not only in the eyes of fo-
reigners both near and remote, but it muft
abate in the eyes of all thofe whom curiofity
has induced to inquire into the grounds of
this profecution. For though the two lead-
ing parties in the laft Parliament agreed to
profecute, they did not agree upon the reafon why they fhould profecute. They cannot agree upon the facts wherewith to charge
him ; for whilft the leader of the impeachment contends that Bengal is ruined by Mr.
Haftings, the India Minifters fay, it is of all
countries the moft flourifhing.*

To

* The leader of the impeachment, in introducing
the firft article to the Houfe of Commons, fuppofes
himfelf fpeaking to Mr. Haftings thus : " I inquire
" not into your particular conduct ; I am fatisfied
" with the refult ; I want not to know if you have
" made two, three, or five hundred thoufand pounds ;
" keep

To conclude. I think I have fully demonstrated, that neither the continuance nor the renovation of the proceedings can be of any public service whatever. It may, for any thing I know to the contrary, serve to promote the politics of some, and to gratify the resentment of others; but there the advantages must stop, for I do bid defiance to the warmest advocate for the prosecution, to point out one possible benefit that can result to this country, or to any other, from Mr.

" keep what you have got; you have made a nume-
" rous people happy; you have increased the com-
" merce of the country, enlarged the means of
" wealth, and improved its revenues; in so doing,
" you have reflected honour and glory on the Bri-
" tish nation." These words were spoken hypothetically, and the inference was, that had the provinces
in India been well governed, and rendered happy and
flourishing, he would not have moved the impeachment. Now we find by the evidence which the Managers themselves called, by the testimony of one of
his Majesty's officers delivered in the House of Commons, and by the votes of the House year after year,
that what was stated hypothetically, is strictly and
literally true; still the impeachment goes on. Who
then will say, that the measures, and not the man,
are the ground of this prosecution ?

N

Haf-

Haftings's acquittal or condemnation. Neither can an acquittal totally reftore the credit of the accufed, for the late Commons have infifted upon the truth and importance of the articles they intended to abandon; neither can the prifoner's condemnation refcue the chief Manager's character from the charge of calumny and falfehood; for the principal crimes he imputed to Mr. Haftings, are not at iffue between him and the Houfe of Commons.

The difcontinuance cannot leffen the dignity of this Houfe of Commons in the eyes of other nations, near or remote; neighbouring kingdoms condemn the tedious fyftem of profecution, and diftant ones have petitioned againft it.

It cannot affect future offenders from the Eaft, for a new and more effectual Court of Judicature is provided.

The torturing of Mr. Haftings may be a ruinous, but cannot be an ufeful example.

It

It may deter future governors abroad, gene-
nerals in the field, and admirals at sea, from
taking vigorous measures to serve their country in the moment of necessity. They will
recollect that there may again exist a minis-
try capable of applauding and punishing one
and the same transaction;* that there may
exist a people, who, while they enjoy the
blessings that are procured for them, can be-
hold with a torpid indifference, the severest
punishment inflicted upon the man to whom
they stand indebted for their enjoyments.

* Mr. Hastings is treated by his countrymen with
more severity than the Spartan youth, who being
alarmed by the noise of an attack made by an enemy
on the city as he was bathing himself, caught up a
weapon and ran naked into the midst of the battle.
The singularity of his appearance made the enemy
believe him to be a god, and the consternation occa-
sioned by such a notion, made them easily desist from
the attack; the Spartans paid the highest compli-
ments to the zeal and bravery of the young man; they
gave him a crown of laurel worth three-pence, and
fined him more than he was worth for going into
battle without a shield. This young man was the
son of that Phœbides, whose ungrateful treatment by
his country I took notice of in the Elucidation.

It

It cannot be of any ufe to this country to profcribe and banifh fuperior virtue as it was to the Athenians. A republic, jealous for its liberty, might juftly apprehend danger from the popularity of an individual, but in a fet-tled government like this, there can be no excufe for political ingratitude.

It is not a duty incumbent upon the pre-fent Houfe of Commons to follow up the refolutions of the laft ; for if that were a re-ceived maxim, it would have been the duty of the laft Parliament to follow up the refo-lutions of their predeceffors againft the then and prefent Minifter. No reafon can be gi-ven why the hyperboles againft Mr. Haf-tings's proceeding from the fame ejacula-ting lips fhould have more weight arid cre-dit, than when they were directed againft the Britifh Minifter.*

Upon

* " Let no man talk of the decaying energies of " nature; all the acts and monuments in the records " of peculation, the confolidated corruption of ages,

the

Upon a queſtion of this kind, it is hoped that every member will exerciſe his own judgment. We all know that in great national queſtions, ſuch as the impoſing of taxes, approving of conventions, and the like, the miniſter muſt be ſupported, or his adminiſtration is at end. But in a queſtion of impeachment, I do not ſee any particular intereſt that a Miniſter can have in its deciſion one way or the other, unleſs he thinks that his own ſtrength conſiſts in the weakneſs of his opponents, and that to render them weak, he muſt make them unpopular. The miniſter, however, may recollect, that what renders the oppoſition unpopular, will not gain him an augmentation of eſteem. That this proſecution has diminiſhed the popula-

---

" the patterns of exemplary plunder in the heroic " times of Roman iniquity, never equalled the gigan- " tic corruption of this ſingle act. Never did Nero, " in all the inſolent prodigality of deſpotiſm, deal out " to his prætorian guards a donation to be named " with the largeſs ſhowered down by our Chancellor " of the Exchequer, on the faithful band of his In- " dian Sepoys." Mr. Burke's Speech in Parliament.

rity of the gentlemen called the oppofition, is a fact beyond all difpute. They feel the effect too fenfibly to deny it ; even the chief Manager has been heard publicly to lament the growing difrepute of the impeachment.

I have now only to requeft the reader to confider what I have written, as coming from a perfon who owes no obligation to Mr. Haftings ; who never efpoufed his caufe through gratitude for paft favours, nor expectation of future ; who, though he courted not his fmiles whilft in the plenitude of his power, and in the exercife of a moft extenfive patronage, has voluntarily and without folicitation joined the ftandard of his defence, in the day of his adverfity.

I here again repeat what I faid in the Elucidation, that I never fhould have written ferioufly on the fubject, had I not found, from every converfation I ever heard concerning the impeachment, that the facts

were

were totally obfcured in the fmoke of invective and aggravation ; but as I was careful in the work above mentioned, to ftate no facts, but what were well authenticated, fo I have been cautious in thefe fheets to advance no propofition that had not the affent of my heart and the fanction of my moft deliberative judgment.—I am not the advocate of Mr. Haftings, but the advocate of juftice, and had I not from frequently attending at Weftminfter Hall, from reading a variety of documents, and from Mr. Haftings's general character in India, ftrengthened by my own obfervations, been fully convinced that his merit infinitely exceeded his demerit, and that the cleareft and moft impartial elucidation of his conduct would be the ftrongeft and moft effectual defence, I never would have written one line in his vindication.

Should this pamphlet attract the notice of the late chief Manager or his affociates, they

they will probably fay of the friends of Mr. Haftings, that the nearer he approaches to his defence, the more they are alarmed for his fafety. This, however, like moft of their affertions, is without foundation.—I difclaim the knowledge of Mr. Haftings's wifhes as to the continuance of the proceedings, but I never looked forward to a future event with a ftronger confidence in the fpirit of prediction than I do to this, namely, that if the prefent Houfe of Commons re-appoint the late chief Manager, they will find that they have granted him an *eftate in profecution*, determinable only with the political lives of the grantors, or with the natural deceafe, either of the granted or of the grantee.

THE END.